SUPER SIMPLE

INDOOR GARDENS

A KID'S GUIDE TO GARDENING

Super Sandcastle

ALEX KUSKOWSKI

An Imprint of Abdo Publishing
www.abdopublishing.com

Consulting Editor, Diane Craig,
M.A./Reading Specialist

SUPER SIMPLE GARDENING

www.abdopublishing.com

Published by Abdo Publishing, a division of ABDO, PO Box 398166, Minneapolis, Minnesota 55439. Copyright © 2015 by Abdo Consulting Group, Inc. International copyrights reserved in all countries. No part of this book may be reproduced in any form without written permission from the publisher. Super SandCastle™ is a trademark and logo of Abdo Publishing.

Printed in the United States of America, North Mankato, Minnesota
102014
012015

Editor: Liz Salzmann
Content Developer: Alex Kuskowski
Cover and Interior Design and Production: Mighty Media, Inc.
Photo Credits: Jen Schoeller, Shutterstock

Library of Congress Cataloging-in-Publication Data

Kuskowski, Alex.
 Super simple indoor gardens : a kid's guide to gardening / Alex Kuskowski.
    pages cm. -- (Super simple gardening)
 ISBN 978-1-62403-524-1
1. Indoor gardening--Juvenile literature. 2. Indoor gardens--Juvenile literature. I. Title.
II. Series: Kuskowski, Alex. Super simple gardening.
 SB419.2.K87 2015
 635.9'65--dc23
            2014023975

Super SandCastle™ books are created by a team of professional educators, reading specialists, and content developers around five essential components—phonemic awareness, phonics, vocabulary, text comprehension, and fluency—to assist young readers as they develop reading skills and strategies and increase their general knowledge. All books are written, reviewed, and leveled for guided reading, early reading intervention, and Accelerated Reader® programs for use in shared, guided, and independent reading and writing activities to support a balanced approach to literacy instruction.

TO ADULT HELPERS

· · · · · · · · · · · · · · ·

Gardening is a lifelong skill. It is fun and simple to learn. There are a few things to remember to keep kids safe. Gardening requires commitment. Help your children stay dedicated to watering and caring for their plants. Some activities in this book recommend adult supervision. Some use sharp tools. Be sure to review the activities before starting and be ready to assist your budding gardeners when necessary.

· · · · · · · · · · · · · · ·

Key Symbols

In this book you may see these symbols. Here is what they mean.

Sharp!
You will be working with a sharp object. Get help.

Inside Light
Put your plant inside.
Direct Light = in sunlight.
Indirect Light = in shade.

TABLE OF CONTENTS

GET INTO GARDENING

Make a plant paradise inside your home. You can grow plants any time of year. Gardening is good for the **environment**. It's fun too!

It is easy to start. This book will give you simple tips. Explore the world of gardening. Get your hands dirty. Grow something great!

INDOOR GARDENS

Indoor gardens are easy to create. You can grow plants year-round indoors. Plant a green letter. Water a **succulent** in a can. Experiment by growing a bean in a jar.

PLANT PLANNING

All indoor gardens take planning.

Plants need care to survive.

Find out how to start!

Inside Gardens

Indoor plants need a safe place. Follow these rules to choose the best area in your home!

- Make sure they won't get knocked over or stepped on.
- Put them where the temperature stays about the same.
- Make sure the plants get sunlight. Put them near a window.

Plant Tip

Set a watering **schedule**. Check the soil to see if your plants need water. Stick a finger into the soil ½ inch (1.3 cm). If it is dry, the plant may need water.

TOOLS

These are some of the important gardening tools you will be using for the projects in this book.

containers & pots

garden gloves

hand trowel

plants

soil & sand

rocks

watering can

spray bottle

SAFETY

Be safe and responsible while gardening. There are a few rules for doing gardening projects.

Ask Permission

Get **permission** to do a project. You might want to use tools or things around the house. Ask first!

Be Safe

Get help from an adult when using sharp tools or moving something heavy.

Clean Up

Clean up your working area when you are finished. Put everything away.

DIG INTO DIRT

Different indoor plants need different kinds of soil. The right soil is the key to growing a good garden.

Choose the best soil for your plants. If you don't know, ask a gardener for help.

Desert Potting Mix

This soil works best with **cacti** and other **succulents**.

All-Purpose Potting Mix

This soil works well with most plants in pots. Buy soil with **peat moss** and **vermiculite**.

ADD IT!

Rocks

Some pots need rocks in the bottom. This helps the water drain out of the soil. It keeps the roots from getting too wet.

Fertilizer

Fertilizer is food for plants! Most plants need fertilizer every few weeks. It comes in **pellets**, powder, or liquid. The package will tell you how much to use.

LOCATION STATION

Find a Spot

Putting your plants in the right place is important! Choose a spot with the right amount of sun.

Pick a Pot

Containers for plants come in all shapes, sizes, and **materials**. Try colorful plastic pots or fun clay pots.

Use the Right Size Pot

Plants need room to grow! The roots should not touch the sides of the pot.

Small Pots
Pots less than 8 inches (20 cm) deep.

Medium Pots
Pots 8 inches (20 cm) to 16 inches (40.5 cm) deep.

Large Pots
Pots deeper than 16 inches (40.5 cm).

COOL CARE

Watering Wisdom

Plants need water. Keep the soil moist for most plants. If the soil feels dry, water your plants!

The Right Light

Light is important! Get the right light for your plants. Check how many hours of sunlight your plants need.

To get the right light, know what direction the windows face. South facing windows give the most light. East and west facing windows have a medium amount of light. North facing windows have the least light.

Prune Your Plants

Plants need to be pruned. Cut off any discolored leaves. Also cut off any dead or dying flowers.

Pest Detective

Check your indoor plants for bugs. Learn about any bugs you find. Find out if they are good or bad for your plants.

PLANT IN A CAN

A GREAT GIFT FOR ANY OCCASION!

CAUTION SHARP!

INSIDE DIRECT SUN

Supplies

- metal can
- dish soap
- measuring tape
- paper
- pencil
- decorative paper
- scissors
- Mod Podge
- foam brush
- small rocks
- hand trowel
- garden gloves
- desert potting soil
- succulent plant
- watering can

DIRECTIONS

1 Clean the can with soap and water. Take off any labels.

2 Measure the height of the can. Write down the measurement. Measure around the can. Add ½ inch (1.3 cm). Write down the total measurement.

3 Cut a piece of paper to match the measurements.

4 Cover the outside of the can with Mod Podge.

Project continues on the next page

5. Wrap the paper around the can.

6. Brush Mod Podge along the edge of the paper. Smooth it down. Let the Mod Podge dry.

7. Put a 1-inch (2.5 cm) layer of rocks in the can.

8 Fill the can halfway with soil.

9 Put the **succulent** plant in the can.

10 Fill around the plant with soil. Press down. Make sure the plant is firm in the soil.

11 Water the plant.

COOL CARE
Water the plant every 1 to 2 weeks. Check to see if the soil is dry. It needs 3 to 5 hours of sun a day.

GROW A LETTER

SPELL IT THE GREEN WAY!

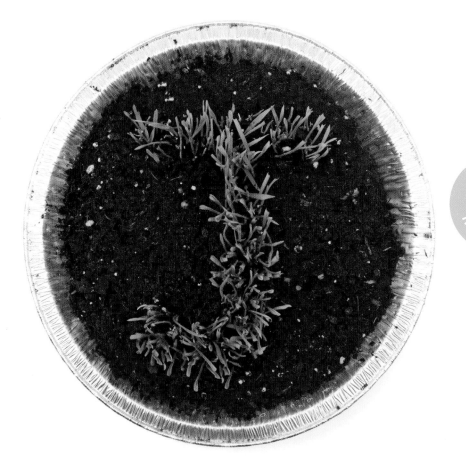

Supplies

INSIDE · INDIRECT SUN

wheatgrass seeds

bowl

watering can

2 aluminum pie tins

pen

small rocks

garden gloves

potting soil

spray bottle

paper

scissors

DIRECTIONS

1. Put the seeds in the bowl. Fill the bowl with water. Let them **soak** 1 hour. Then empty out the water.

2. Use a pen to make three holes in one pie tin.

3. Cover the bottom of the tin with a layer of rocks.

4. Fill the tin with potting soil. Spray the soil with water until it is wet.

Project continues on the next page

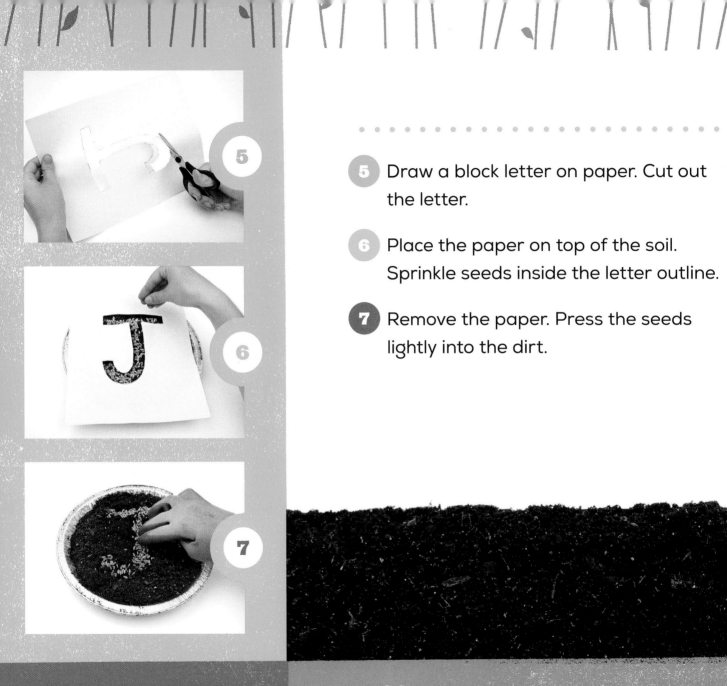

5 Draw a block letter on paper. Cut out the letter.

6 Place the paper on top of the soil. Sprinkle seeds inside the letter outline.

7 Remove the paper. Press the seeds lightly into the dirt.

8. Cover the seeds with a thin layer of soil.

9. Water the seeds with the spray bottle.

10. Cover the seeds with the other pie tin for 2 days. Then take off the top tin. Put the grass in a sunny area. Spray it with water every day.

COOL CARE Keep watering every day. When the grass reaches 6 inches (15 cm), trim it with scissors.

MINI DESERT

MAKE A DESERT FOR YOUR ROOM!

INSIDE
DIRECT SUN

Supplies

• • • • • • • • •

medium pot

small rocks

desert potting soil

hand trowel

garden gloves

2 succulents,
2 inches (5 cm) tall

2.5-inch (6 cm)
grafted cactus

sand

plastic zipper bag

scissors

watering can

DIRECTIONS

1. Cover the bottom of the pot with small rocks.

2. Add desert potting soil. Fill the pot to a few inches from the top.

3. Dig a small hole. Take a **succulent** out of its tray. Pull on the bottom to loosen the roots.

Project continues on the next page

4 Put the plant in the hole. Pat the soil around the plant.

5 Dig another small hole. Place the second **succulent** in it. Pat the soil around the plant.

6 Dig a third hole. Very carefully take the **cactus** out of its tray. Avoid the sharp points!

7 Pull on the bottom to loosen the roots. Place the cactus in the third hole.

8 Add more soil. Pat the soil around all of the plants.

9 Put sand in a plastic zipper bag. Cut one bottom corner of the bag.

10 Pour the sand out through the hole. Cover the soil with sand. Add rocks.

11 Water your desert and put it in a sunny spot. The plants need 3 hours of sun a day.

COOL CARE

Once a week, stick a finger below the sand into the soil. If the soil is dry, the plants need water.

CRAZY BEANS

GROW A BEAN WITHOUT SOIL!

Supplies

· · · · · · · · ·

INSIDE
DIRECT SUN

small glass jar

paper towels

1 bean seed

spray bottle

garden gloves

hand trowel

potting soil

small pot

DIRECTIONS

1. Fill the jar with water. Pour the water out. Leave the jar wet.

2. Fill the jar with wet paper towels.

3. Push the bean between the towels and the glass.

4. Put the jar near a sunny window.

Project continues on the next page

5 Use a spray bottle to water the bean every day.

6 In about 10 days, the bean seed will have a stem and roots. Carefully take the bean plant out of the jar.

7 Fill the small pot with potting soil.

8 Make a small hole with your finger.

9 Put the bean plant's roots in the hole.

10 Cover the roots with soil. Pat the soil to make it firm.

11 Water your bean plant!

COOL CARE Water the plant every 2 to 3 days. Keep in a spot that gets 3 hours of sun every day.

GLOSSARY

cactus – a plant with sharp spikes instead of leaves that grows in hot dry places.

container – something that other things can be put into.

environment – nature and everything in it, such as the land, sea, and air.

fertilizer – something used to make plants grow better in soil.

material – something that other things can be made of, such as clay, plastic, or metal.

peat moss – a type of moss that usually grows on wet land and is used in gardening.

pellet – a small, hard ball.

permission – when a person in charge says it's okay to do something.

saucer – a shallow dish that goes under something to catch spills.

schedule – a list of the times when things will happen.

soak – to remain covered in a liquid for a while.

succulent – a plant, such as a cactus or an aloe, that has thick stems or leaves that store water.

vermiculite – a light material that holds water that is often added to potting soil.